I0821728

Platypus

by Grace Hansen

Abdo Kids Jumbo is an Imprint of Abdo Kids
abdobooks.com

abdobooks.com

Published by Abdo Kids, a division of ABDO, P.O. Box 398166, Minneapolis, Minnesota 55439.

Printed in China

052019

092019

Photo Credits: Alamy, Getty Images, iStock, Minden Pictures, National Geographic Image Collection, Science Source, Shutterstock

Production Contributors: Teddy Borth, Jennie Forsberg, Grace Hansen
Design Contributors: Dorothy Toth, Pakou Moua

Library of Congress Control Number: 2018963343

Publisher's Cataloging-in-Publication Data

Names: Hansen, Grace, author.

Title: Platypus / by Grace Hansen.

Description: Minneapolis, Minnesota : Abdo Kids, 2020 | Series: Australian animals | Includes online resources and index.

Identifiers: ISBN 9781532185458 (lib. bdg.) | ISBN 9781532186431 (ebook) | ISBN 9781532186929 (Read-to-me ebook)

Subjects: LCSH: Platypus--Juvenile literature. | Marsupials--Juvenile literature. | Animals--Australia--Juvenile literature.

Classification: DDC 599.29--dc23

Table of Contents

Platypus

Platypuses live in eastern Australia. They also live on the nearby island of Tasmania.

Platypuses can be found near or in fresh water, like lakes, streams, and rivers. Many live in the Murray or Darling Rivers.

The platypus is a very **unique mammal**. It has a flat head and a duck-like bill. The bill is covered in a leathery skin.

Its body grows up to 22 inches (55.9 cm) long. It ends in a short, wide tail.

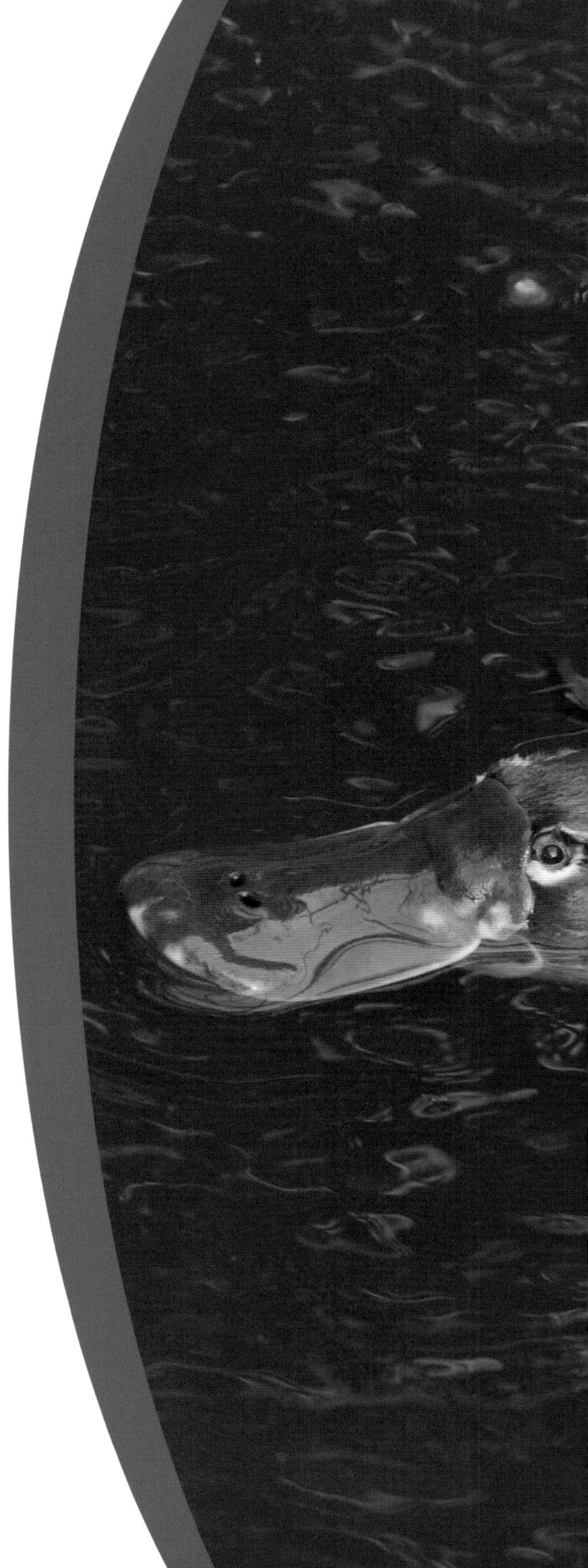

A platypus's back is covered in brown fur. Lighter fur covers the belly.

Its **webbed** feet help the platypus swim. Its long claws help it dig burrows.

Burrows

Platypus burrows are found near fresh water. Platypuses sleep around 17 hours a day in their burrows.

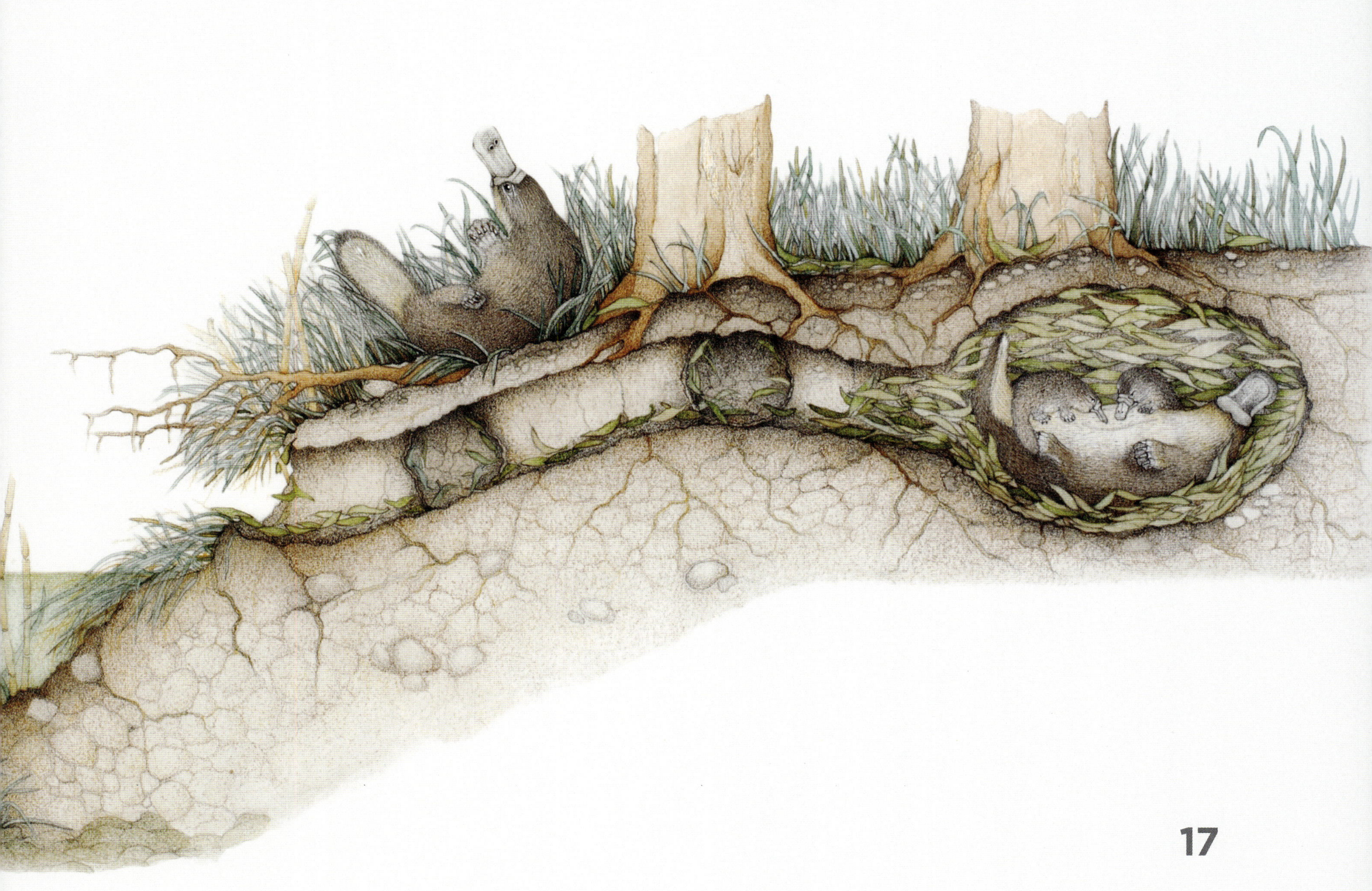

Food & Hunting

At night, platypuses come out to hunt and eat. They like to eat insects, snails, worms, and more!

Baby Platypuses

Unlike many **mammals**, platypuses lay eggs. **Females** lay 1 to 3 eggs at a time. Babies stay in the burrow until they are around 4 months old.

More Facts

- **Male** platypuses have a spur on their back ankles. The spurs contain venom that is strong enough to kill small animals.
- Platypus venom will not likely kill humans. But it will cause intense pain that can last for weeks.
- Platypuses store the food they catch underwater in their cheeks. They eat the food once they get above water.

Glossary

female – an animal that produces eggs or gives birth to live young.

male – an animal that fathers, rather than births, its young.

mammal – a warm-blooded animal with fur or hair on its skin and a skeleton inside its body. Mammal mothers make milk to feed their babies.

unique – being the only of its type

webbed – having toes connected by a membrane.

Index

Visit **abdokids.com** to access crafts, games, videos, and more!

Use Abdo Kids code

APK5458

or scan this QR code!